THE
SISTINE CHAPEL

art courses

ATS Italia Editrice

Summary

On the right:
Entrance to the Sistine Chapel,
Swiss Guards to the fore

Introduction

The Sistine Chapel, one of the most significant places of Christianity as it is a papal Chapel and seat of the conclave (assembly of cardinals who elect the new pontiff) preserves works of art, considered among the highest artistic expressions of western civilization. At the end of the XV century the most important Italian painters worked here. Here Michelangelo frescoed two masterpieces: the ceiling with the stories of the creation of the world (1508-1512) and the end wall with the Last Judgement (1536-1541).

The chapel derives its name from its first client, Pope Sixtus IV della Rovere (1471-1484) who wanted to restore the old Papal Chapel, called "Cappella Magna".

The realization of the great work of art began in 1474 and ended in 1483 when the chapel dedicated to the Virgin Assumption was solemnly inaugurated by the Pope on the 15th August. Architect Baccio Pontelli's plan reused the mediaeval walls up to a third of their height and the same plan was realized by Mino da Fiesole, both artists from Florence. According to some experts the size of the hall (40.93 meters long, 13.40 m. wide and 20.70 m. high) is the same as the Temple of Solomon in Jerusalem, destroyed in 70 A.D. by the Romans.

The main entrance is situated on the opposite side of the small entrance which is nowadays used as access point, and it is preced-ed by the monumental Sala Regia, used for audiences.

Light enters through arched windows (arched in the upper part); a slightly lowered barrel vault is connected to the side walls through lunettes and triangular caps. On the right side the refined choir stalls were the site of the choir, while the stone bench on the three sides of the chapel was used by papal dignitaries. A big marble balustrade, topped by candelabrums, divides the area for the clergy from that of the public: in the second half of the 16th c. it was restored to its original position to widen the first area. The magnificent "cos-

matesque" mosaic floor completes the decoration.

In 1481, Sixtus IV commissioned Pietro Perugino from Umbria and the most famous Florentine artists (Botticelli, Ghirlandaio, Cosimo Rosselli and Signorelli) to decorate the side walls. They worked with their pupils like Biagio d'Antonio Tucci, Bartolomeo della Gatta and Luca Signorelli. Pier Matteo d'Amelia had to paint the vault with a star spangled sky.

Sixtus IV's nephew, Giuliano della Rovere, who was to become Pope Julius II (1503-1513), had to change the pictorial decorations inside the chapel. So, in order to renew the magnificent city, he called on Michelangelo Buonarroti (1475-1564), artist already known in Florence, who had worked for him before. Michelangelo accepted, with some contrasts, to decorate the vault using "frescoing". The work was completed in four years of hard work, from 1508 to 1512.

The Vault represents the story of humanity before Christ. In the big architectonical painted structure nine stories from the Genesis are located. They are in a frame flanked by "naked men" (Ignudi). Prophets and Sybils seat on monumental thrones at the sides of the main panels, between the "vele"(sails); they are forecasting Christ's coming. Michelangelo represents the stories of four Biblical heroes in the big "pennacchi" (penaches) in the corners (David, Ester, Judith and Moses). You can read in their undertakings God's intervention for chosen people's salvation. Michelangelo paints in the "lunette" and "vele" Christ's Ancestors flanking Sybils and Prophets. Michelangelo follows the genealogy from the first chapter of the Gospel according to St. Matthew. The whole story of the Salvation is represented in the complicated iconographic program, where, according to some critics, theologians of the Papal Court contributed. These characters , represented some time in little groups, are the link with the lower panels by the painters of the XV century: Moses symbolizes the Old Testament, and Jesus, central point of the history of Salvation and founder of the saved mankind, thanks to his death and resurrection. According to the theological Renaissance thought, you can read the ceiling of the Sistine Chapel like a magnificent celebration of God's work when He moulded Adam in his own image and likeness, and setting him in the center of all the created things, thanks to the mystery of Incarnation, he is elevated to become God's Son.

The fresco on the altar wall representing the Last Judgement was executed later by the same artist who worked there from 1536 to 1541, commissioned by Pope Paul III Farnese (1534-1549), who had in turn confirmed the job commissioned by his predecessor Pope Clement VII (1523-1534). Accurate restorations and cleanings, begun in the year 1980 by experts from the Restoration Workshop of the Vatican Museum (Laboratorio di Restauro), brought the paintings to their ancient splendour (the Vault, then the Last Judgement, and the side walls with the frescoes executed by the 15th c painters). It was a world-known event, due to the technique used and the final results.

The Restoration of the Sistine Chapel Frescoes

The restoration of Michelangelo's frescoes in the Sistine Chapel represents the natural sequel to the work carried out between 1964 and 1974 on the fifteenth century "Histories of Moses and of Christ" on the side walls, and again between 1979 and 1980 on the sixteenth century repainting of the two biblical episodes on the entrance wall.

The cleaning of Michelangelo's ceiling was to have followed that of the series of portraits of the Popes, but the conditions noted in the lunette of "Eleazar Mathan" – in particular the presence of numerous micro-tears in the painted surface – advised against further delay, and between 1980 and 1984 the fourteen lunettes with the "Ancestor of Christ" were cleaned, together with the "Popes" by Perugino, Ghirlandaio, Botticelli and Cosimo Rosselli.

The damage proved to be the result of variations in temperature and humidity, causing contractions in the layer of glue which during past restorations had been applied to the painted surface as a varnish in order to revive the colours, darkened and dulled by the gradual build-up of deposits of dust and candle-black that the methods of cleaning generally used – bread, sour wine and water – were not able to sufficiently lighten. The restoration revealed a pure colour, full of iridescent effects, and very similar to that brought to light by the careful restoration of the "Doni Tondo", also being carried out at that time. And yet it was unexpected, and consequently raised doubts and incredulity in some critics, causing the fierce polemic that for a time accompanied the work.

Following this first period of work, the cleaning of the ceiling itself took place between 1985 and 1989 and confirmed the results of the restoration of the lunettes. Finally, from the spring of 1990.

work went ahead on the "Last Judgement", revealing yet again a rich source of new knowledge.

As we know, every restoration provides a rich and almost inexhaustible source of information about the functioning of the creative process and gives clues and solutions to problems of dating, iconography and style relating to the creation of the work of art. If this is true in general, it is all the more so in the case of Michelangelo's frescoes, where the smoke, dust, dirt and restorations of nearly five centuries had deposited a patina, which, if not noble, was undoubtedly suggestive, giving rise to the myth of an artist who technically lacked preparation. The cleaning of the ceiling has, however, revealed the work of a typical Renaissance artist, a sculptor by vocation, a reluctant painter and architect, with a technical background and artistic preparation that enabled him, despite his apparent inexperience, to tackle the most monumental challenge that an artist had ever faced, creating a work of exceptional skill both in terms of formal perfection and of technical achievement, the equivalent of a treatise on mural painting. True to his Florentine origins, Michelangelo painted in "buon fresco", gradually eliminating from his palette – perhaps because of problems of 'mould' in the early stages – those colours like red lead that required the use of a binding medium. The use of "fresco secco" was limited to retouching and to the monochrome medallions at the feet of the "Ignudi". From the point of view of technique of execution, all the methods employed – in particular the use of enamel and lapislazuli in fresco – came from the workshop of Domenico Ghirlandaio, where Michelangelo served his apprenticeship, and from where he summoned most of the assistants who worked with him in the early stages of the work: Bugiardini, Jacopo di Sandro – with whom he immediately came into conflict – Jacopo di Lazzaro Torni known as Indaco Vecchio, who took the latter'place in January 1509, and his child-hood friend, Granacci, who had introduced him to the bottega of Ghirlandaio.

Michelangelo could certainly not have learnt, during the brief stay of these 'assistants' on the scaffolding, the difficult technique of painting in true fresco; they helded to 'freshen up' the knowledge assimilated during his apprenticeship with Ghirlandaio. They assisted in the layout of the work and painted not only the decorative elements of the cornices but also – under the rigid and constant control of the master – some of the figures of the stories of Noah. We note their presence in the different modes of painting and, often, in the sudden lowering of quality compared to the parts by Michelangelo which, even in the early stages, are of a constantly high level, unattainable by any other artist.

The assistants worked with him until the autumn of 1509 when the scale of the figures and the rhythms of the composition in the "Fall of Man" made it impossible for them to work with him on the scaffolding in any way that was even partially autonomous. So Michelangelo sent home the more able of his assistants – Granacci and Bugiardini in particular – above all because, according to the contract, all the expenses fell to him and there was no sense in keeping them if he could not put them to good use.

The decoration has also substantiated the fact, indicated by the chronicles and letters, that there was a pause in the work in the summer of 1510, immediately after Michelangelo had painted the "Creation of Eve", below which stood significantly the marble screen separating the laity from the clergy. It has also shown that once work started again in the autumn of 1511, the pace accelerated remarkably, so that, for example, the lunette of "Rehoboam and Abjijah" and the scene of the "Separation of light from darkness" were painted in one day. One reason for this acceleration was probably the use, in the scenes from Genesis in the centre of the ceiling and of the groups of figures in the spandrels, of the indirect impression, dispensing with the pouncing of the "spolvero" as used almost everywhere in the first series of frescoes. As a result of the cleaning, the influence that Michelangelo had on his contemporaries becomes more than evident. It can be seen in Raphael and his entourage – particularly Giulio Romano – as

Michelangzelo, Last Judgement,
detail: Christ the Judge (during clean-up operations)

well as in the so-called Florentine Mannerism of Rosso, Pontormo, Andrea del Sarto and Beccafumi, who were influenced not only in formal terms but also – and this was not noted before – by his use of colour.

It was a very different artist who painted the "Last Judgement" little more than twenty years later. Technically Michelangelo executed his composition in "buon fresco" as before on the ceiling, but here his palette is richer and, alongside the usual earth colours, we find pigments such as red lake, "giallolino" and orpiment. For the blue of the sky he freely used the very expensive lapislazuli, most probably chosen because here it was no longer the artist who bore the expense but the Pope. Apart from this detail the use of lapislazuli is fundamental, for it determines the generally much warmer tone, clearly a result of the artist's changing sensibility, influenced undoubtedly both by his familiarity over a period of twenty years with the work of Sebastiano del Piombo and by a journey to Venice made in 1529.

Although essentially Florentine by training, Michelangelo turned in his later works to new ideas that in terms of light and colour came from the Venetian School, showing his awareness of the outside world and his lack of prejudice towards a cultural environment about which, in words at least, he expressed many reservations.

THE SISTINE CHAPEL

A GLOBAL VIEW

Pope Sisto IV della Rovere (1471-1484) wanted the most important painters of the end of 1400 to fresco the side walls of the Chapel of the papal palace.

Botticelli, Ghirlandaio, Piero di Cosimo, Cosimo Rosselli, Perugino and Pinturicchio together with their pupils started painting the side walls of the chapel after October 27, 1481 when they signed the contract. The side walls are divided into three orders horizontally, two very elegant orders pilaster strips divide vertically the panels.

In the lower level there are the sham tapestries with the Pope's coat of arms.

Along the second level, that is the most important one, scenes from the Bible are represented: if you face the altar you have, on the left, scenes from the Old Testament (the Life of Moses). On the right, scenes from the New Testament with the Life of Christ.

The fresco paintings are clearly executed to compare the life of Moses and Christ, the two men who set Israel's people free, and Jesus Christ, the Redeemer not only of the Israelites, but also of mankind.

The inscriptions up above the frescoes are the titles of the scenes. The panels gather and melt different happenings so that it is quite difficult to split the precise interpretation of the episodes from the Bible.

In the upper level, where the windows are located, we have 28 out of 32 original Pope's images in the monochrome niches. The "Ceiling" and the "Judgement" complete the Sistine Chapel and testify the determinant contribution given by Michelangelo's daring perception of his art.

The Sistine Chapel can be considered one of the most significative and complete testimonies of the story of Salvation narrated in the Bible. All this can be resumed in the Creator's figure and his Son, the Supreme Judge of history. Michelangelo dedicates the most beautiful images of the Chapel to these two figures.

THE FIFTEENTH-CENTURY ARTISTS

PIETRO PERUGINO: MOSES' JOURNEY TO EGYPT

The happenings from the life of the Redeemer of the Jewish people from the slavery in Egypt started from the end wall with the fresco with Moses rescued from the floods of the river Nile. The fresco was cancelled by Michelangelo's Last Judgement. Today the Stories about Moses start with the description of the journey to Egypt. As a whole the composition and some portraits can be ascribed to Perugino (1445-50/1523), who used some of his best scholars.

The scenes of this panel refer to the biblical narration about the book of the Exodus (4,18-26). Pease note on the bottom right the representation of the rite of Moses son's circumcision.

SANDRO BOTTICELLI AND HIS SCHOLARS: "MOSES' PROOFS"

"Moses' proofs" are the subject of this fresco painted by the Florentine painter Sandro Botticelli (1445-1510) and his scholars. The panel is one of the most complex because of the many represented episodes: the killing by Moses of an Egyptian, who struck an Hebrew (on the right); the flight, after the killing, to Madian; then Moses meets and defends some local girls (Ietro's daughters), because some shepherds don't let them water their herd. Moses will choose among them his wife, Sefora. (Exodus, 2,11-20); up above on the left, Moses gets off his shoes because of a God's order who appears from a burning bush. God tells him to go back to Egypt to free the people of Israel; bottom left, Moses and his family's journey. These episodes are told in the biblical book of the Exodus in the chapters 2, 3 and 4. Botticelli's elegance and charm are evident in the two female figures in the center of the panel.

BIAGIO D'ANTONIO: THE CROSSING OF THE RED SEA

The episodes painted by Biagio d'Antonio Tucci (1446-1516) are the less important, from an artistic point of view. The biblical episode is very well known: Moses and his people are running away from Egypt; Pharaoh's army is running after them. They can cross the Red Sea because God opens a passage through the water. The same water will close on the Egyptians who will drown together with their horses (Exodus, 14, 23-30). The woman on her knee, near Moses' feet, who is singing and playing a lyre, is the symbol of Israel who sings and rejoices for the liberation that God has reserved to his people:
"The Lord is my strenght and my hymn, He saved me. He is my Lord and I want to praise him, He is my father's Lord and I want to exalt him!" (Exodus, 15, 2).

COSIMO ROSSELLI: THE CONSIGNMENT OF THE TABLES OF THE LAW

The represented episodes want to resume the happenings told in the book of the Exodus, chiefly the Consignment of the Tables of the Law to Moses. The event is painted up in the center of the fresco, while a little lower Moses' wrath is represented. He has discovered his people worshipping a golden calf and for this reason he breaks the Tables of the Law, and makes the gulty murder, you can notice up above on the right. God gives his people the Law, through Moses, to give a further sign of alliance.

SANDRO BOTTICELLI: PUNISHMENT OF CORE, DATAN E ABIRAM

The episodes painted by Botticelli (whose portrait should be the second figure on the right) is narrated in the biblical text of the book of the Numbers, chapter 16. Core, Datan e Abiram were priests. They rebelled against Moses and questioned Moses and Aronne the religious and political power over the Chosen People. God punishes them by making them be swallowed up by a chasm. The episode is rare to find in the biblical iconography and confirms the Papal authority and underlines how serious are the gestures of those who don't respect the authority of God's priests. To underline the assertion, the Supreme Priest Aronne wears the Tiara, symbol of the Pope, and the Latin inscription on the top of the arch proclaims: "Nobody arrogates to himself honour if he is not called by God".

NEMO·SIBI·ASSVMM
AT·HONORE·M·NIS
VOCATVS·ADEO
TANQVAM·ARON

LUCA SIGNORELLI AND BARTOLOMEO DELLA GATTA: MOSES' WILL AND DEATH

This fresco was mostly painted by Luca Signorelli (1445-1523). Some episodes from the last moments of Moses' life are represented: on the left, Moses giving the rod to Joshua (Deuteronomy, 31); on the right Moses giving the blessing to Israel sons (Deuteronomy, 33). Up above: an Angel pointing out the Promised Land and on the left Moses' death when he was, according to the Bible, 120 years old. (Deuteronomy, 34, 5-6).

The pictorial cycle about Moses' life ends on the wall where the big entrance is located with "The quarrel around Moses' corpse". Originally the fresco was by Signorelli, but it was painted again by Matteo da Lecce in 1560 because of a structural sinking of the wall.

PIETRO PERUGINO: THE BAPTISM OF CHRIST

As well as Moses' stories this painting is the second of the original series that started with the Nativity, that was cancelled and replaced by the Last Judgment by Michelangelo.

The author is Perugino, who perhaps had to coordinate in general the works in the Chapel. The inscription that testifies the attribution of the work to the Umbrian master has been recently brought to the light. He worked together with Pinturicchio.

In the panel are represented episodes from the Gospel according to Matthew. On the left Jesus proclaims to the disciples, on the right John the Baptist is proclaiming. Close up in the centre, Jesus and John at the Baptism are again represented.

SANDRO BOTTICELLI:
THE TEMPTATIONS AND THE PURIFICATION OF THE LEPER

The Temptations of Christ, that is the title of the fresco, seems to leave the main spot to the leper's purification, that is an episode from the Gospel according to Matthew (1, 40), but without any reference to the subject of the painting. Some elements in the fresco, like the façade of the Santo Spirito (Holy Spirit) Hospital instead of the ancient temple of Jerusalem, solves the question. Everything was like a present from Botticelli to the Pope who wanted to build that Hospital, the same Pope who wanted the Sistine Chapel, Pope Sixtus IV. The temptations of Christ (Matthew 4,1-11) are represented in the background. After forty fasting days alone in the desert, the Devil tries to tempt Him in adoration.

DOMENICO GHIRLANDAIO: THE CALLING OF THE FIRST APOSTLES

"Jesus was walking along the sea of Galilea when He saw two brothers, Simone named Pietro, and Andrea. They were throwing their nets in the sea. He told them: "Follow me, I'll let you fish men" They immediately followed Him" (Matthew 4, 18-22).

The calling of Pietro and Andrea is represented in a long landscape that goes in a far horizon and then the calling of other two brothers, Giacomo and Giovanni. They will be the first four out of the twelve Apostles that will share with Jesus every single moment of his life and they will be the privileged observers of His death and His resurrection.

COSIMO ROSSELLI: SERMON ON THE MOUNT

The "Sermon on the Mount" (Matthew 5, 1-12) in which Christ tells the Nine Beatitudes is in close connection with the fresco about "The Consignment of the Tables of the Law". The old law given to Moses by God on the Sinai is now changed in the new law of the Beatitudes told by the Redeemer. In the center is represented the episode that gives the fresco its title, on the right a leper's recovery is represented; it's the miracle that the Lord does when he comes back from the mountain, surrounded by those who listened to His precepts. (Matthew, 8, 1-4).
This is only the first of long series miracles in the gospel according to St. Matthew. Jesus is actually the Redeemer: not only he pronounces words that fill men's soul with fervour, but he demonstrates his divinity thanks to the miracles and he underlines his will to save mankind.

PIETRO PERUGINO: THE CONSIGNEMENT OF THE KEYS

The keys that Christ gives to St. Peter are the symbol of the spiritual power and of the Church and Pope's service. One key is made out of gold, symbolizing the power to judge, the other one is made from silver, symbolizing the power to share good and evil. The ancient world is recalled to our minds thanks to two big Roman arches; they are almost copies of Constantine's arch in Rome, they are flanking a renaissance-style temple of Jerusalem. The new world is represented thanks to the moment in which Jesus gives the keys. The ancient and the new worlds harmonize and underline the historical continuity. The huge open space emphasizes the huge perspective thanks to the lines of the floor; how to show the centrality of this fresco between all the others in the Sistine Chapel.

COSIMO ROSSELLI AND BIAGIO D'ANTONIO: THE LAST SUPPER

The Last Supper is Rosselli's masterpiece. The scene takes place in a wide polygonal room realised with perspective precision. We have a back view of Giuda, the apostle who is going to betray the Lord, and his aureola is not shining like the others apostles'. A little devil on his shoulder symbolizes the temptation to which he is going to yield. On the background the episodes of the Jesus' captivity and the Crucifixion are represented in a kind of window opened on the happenings that should happen soon after the last supper. Take notice of the lively animals represented in the panel.

The cycle closes on the entrance wall with the Resurrection of Christ, the fresco painted in the XVI c. by the Dutch painter Hendrik van den Broek to replace Ghirlandaio's panel, destroyed in 1522, for the falling of the architrave.

LINE OF THE POPES

In the area among the windows, inside the very elegant niches, 28 portraits of the first pontiffs are represented. They are represented in a full-lenght portrait and dressed in liturgical clothing.

It is likely that on the altar wall Christ and Peter were represented in the center and they were flanked by two of Peter's precedessors Lino and Cleto, now they are covered by Michelangelo's Judgment.

The are ascribed to the same artists of Moses and Christ's stories: Botticelli, Perugino, Ghirlandaio and Cosimo Rosselli.

The succession of the Popes is not lined on one wall, but alternates with the opposite wall. Inside a monochrome niche each pope holds a book and papyr (or blessing). Under every figure we can read the pope's name.

Popes Marcellus and Eutychian

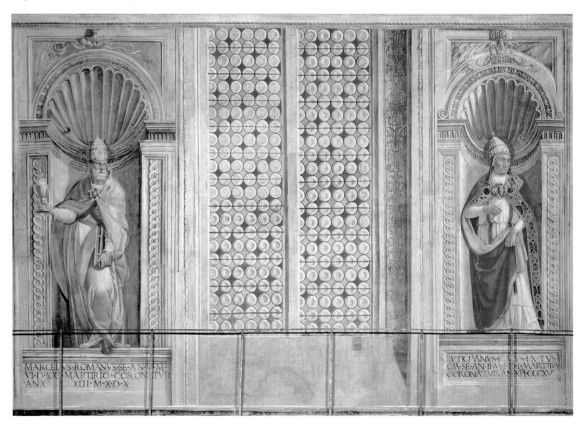

Pope Pius I

THE CEILING

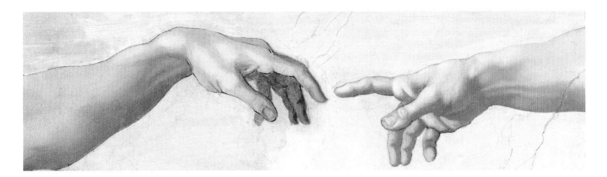

To complete the intuition of the artists who worked to the first decoration of the Sistine Chapel we miss the last artist. That artist is Michelangelo. Pope Giulio II commissioned Michelangelo to paint the ceiling.

It was 1508, Michelangelo was only 33 years old and had no experience as a painter and even less in the fresco technique. The artist worked hard and alone for four years and produced a magnificent synthesis that starts from the Creation to finish with the promise of the Redemption: more than 300 figures are represented in what can be considered a painted architecture, where the strong rinascimental perspective has no importance, differently from the frescos below by the painters of the XV century. There are nine panels in the center we can divide into three groups of three panels each; here the story of the Genesis is narrated, the first book from the Bible. God as the Creator is the subject of the first three panels. The panels of the second group are reserved to Adam and Eve. Adam and Eve's nudity is a strong reference to the Innocence before the disobedience to God. In the last three panels, that are centered on Noah's figure and on the Flood, the represented episodes underline that mankind is ineluctably slave to the Sin.

The tragedy of men's sin seems to take form in twenty naked men represented at the sides of the panels with their exasperated vitality and in the expressions, that go from the dumb contemplation to the desperate shout. The Prophets and Sybils, immediately below the mock cornice, testify the everlasting waiting for the Redemption of humanity. Michelangelo paints the series of Christ's Ancestors in the eight triangular spaces that flank Prophets and Sybils and in the lunettes of the windows: the idea of Messiah that the Prophets preannounce is now historical truth and every Ancestor is a chapter of a story that starts from the moment of the Sin. The artist paints four significant moments from the history of Israel in the triangular spaces in the corners of the Chapel, called "pennacchi"; they symbolize God's presence in his people's everyday's life and the renewal of the promise. These happenings are also linked to the walls below and the themes they express. The Sistine seems to have its logical and final composition and the story of the Salvation is told in its whole.

Above:
Michelangelo,
Ignudi of the Sacrifice of Noah with medallions, a detail

On the right:
Michelangelo,
Ignudo above Prophet Jeremiah, a detail

SEPARATION OF LIGHT FROM DARKNESS

"God said: "Light". And the Light was. He saw that Light was a good thing and separated the light from the darkness and named the day and the night. (Genesis 1, 3-5). God is represented in a great effectual perspective view. He is suspended in the air and with one hand drives darkness away, the other hand origins Light that comes out from his body.

The whole scene is dominated by a strong movement, as if a strong wind was blowing. God's Spirit is often described in the Bible like an "impetuous wind" (Atti 2.2). Michelangelo seems to allude to the presence of the Holy Ghost in the act of the Creation thanks to the whirling that collides with the mantle and the tunic of God Father.

CREATION OF THE STARS AND OF THE PLANTS

"God said: I want lights in the sky to recognize day and night... God saw what he had done and He saw it was a good thing" (Genesis 1 14-15.31).
God is represented twice in this fresco: one is facing us, in the other he is depicted from behind. This last figure gives the scene a sense of a circular movement. God not only creates, but he looks at what he has just created going around to discover the goodness in it and to receive the kindness back. This is a sign of his love for all the things.
Michelangelo turns to the representation of God hanging in space, to express his creative ideas like the previous and following frescoes.

SEPARATION OF WATER FROM THE EARTH

"The earth had no shape and was desolate. Darkness was over the abyss and God's Spirit fluttered over the oceans. God said: The water under the sky must stay in an only place, and the Earth must appear. That's what happened. God named earth the dry places and sea the water" (Genesis 1,2.9-10)

The iconography of the previous centuries imagined a static, majestic and solemn God. Michelangelo breaks the schemes: God is the Creator of life, everything is movement and almighty gesture. The angels and the mantel swollen by the wind that holds him, accentuate the idea of the beauty of creator.

CREATION OF ADAM

"God said: I'll create man in my own image and likeness" (Genesis 1, 26).
God is represented in the classical way, he is an old man with a long fluent white beard, to give the idea of everlasting. Adam is laying down in the new creature's beauty and vigour. It's the moment in which life takes hold of his body. The scene is centered in God's glance that meets Adam's glance and in the two hands: Father's hand is strong and mighty and the first man's hand is opening to underline the opening of life.
The female figure with the afraid expression that appears under the Creator's arm is identified with Eve by some art historians, "as all the living creatures' Mother".

CREATION OF EVE

"God made Adam sleep; He took a rib and closed the skin. God created the woman from Adam's rib and led the woman to the man" (Genesis 2, 21 – 22). The whole scene gravitates round the God's gesture that with his hands invites Eve to come out from Adam's body, while Adam is sound asleep.

Eve's hands are joined to thank, her mouth is a little opened to underline her astonishment and the wonder of the first moment of life, the body is inclined in adoration. All these attitudes show the total beauty of God's gesture, who creates only for love.

THE ORIGINAL SIN

"Eve saw the tree was good to eat...she ate it and then she gave her husband too... they opened their eyes end saw they were naked.... ".
(Genesis 3, 6 - 7).
Adam and Eve are represented on the left with the faces and bodies of innocence, but they are going to receive the fruit that will sign the beginning of their damnation. But the most dramatic element is the withered trunk generated by Eve's body; it symbolizes the experience of death entering, thanks to Sin, in the history. Michelangelo paints on the right of the fresco the ancestors after the Sin. Eve's beautiful shining face is turned into a mask of terror where fear and woe rule. The intention of this is that all the ills of life start from the Original Sin.

NOAH'S SACRIFICE

"Noah came out from the ark with his sons and his wife and his sons' wives, he made an altar to the Lord and made offerings" (Genesis 8,18).

The scene represents the contrast among men's and animals movement and agitation and Noah's quietness; Noah is painted with his eyes closed to es-trange him from the confusion round him. His arm is lifted and his fingers point up. His attitude brings us back to the main meaning: the sacrifice is the gesture that admits God's supremacy over the whole created things and it is a tribute of praise and gratitude to Him, the owner of the destiny of History.

THE FLOOD

"The rain lasted 40 days: waters grew and lifted up Noah's ark.... all the living beings on the earth died". (Genesis 7, 17 – 21).

The fresco is painted with a remarkable realism. The boat that risks sinking because of the elevated number of people that try to take it by assault, is the symbol of the tragedy. People with few possessions try to bring themselves to safety on the rocks and on the earth still emerging from the flood. In the background is Noah's Ark. Noah appears from a little side window, he looks at the sky and with his lifted hand seems to test the consistency of rain. The architectonical structure of the Ark alludes to the idea of a cathedral. The link to the Church as "Ark of Salvation" is evident.

THE DRUNKENNESS OF NOAH

"Noah was drunk, and he laid down naked in his tent" (Genesis 9, 20 and following).

The drunkenness of Noah, who is covered with the mantle by his sons, is the symbol of humanity, slave to Sin. The incapacity to understand and to will is typical of that man who is drunk and it represents the impossibility to approach the truth if you are in Sin.

The male figure who works hard to break up the background (on the left of the panel) is allusive to the rest of Genesis (3, 17), where the hard work is another sign of God's curse on earth after Sin.

The naked men (Ignudi)

The scenes from the Genesis are surrounded by the "naked men"; they are immense male figures with powerful builds referred to mankind's beauty; man that was made in God's own image and likeness. They are sitting on marble cubes and are painted in fixed solemn postures. They put up ribbons, to which big bronze monochrome medallions golden lighted are tied; they represent scenes from the Old Testament. The noteworthy compositive function of these figures had different interpretations: geniuses of the Golden Age, wingless Angel, Michelangelo's neo-platonic expressions. They break the continuity among the architectonic structures and link the different panel of the Genesis.

They are represented in a variety of bodily positions and spiritual expressions; they are represented in different attitudes to relive the whole and capture our attention.

The wonderful architectonical structure painted by Michelangelo turns the vault into an illusory space in which the elements gain a new relief, almost three-dimensional: the harmonious bodies are intentionally put in different postures to mask the different points of view, the only incongruence of Michelangelo's complicated architectonical structure.

Below: Ignudi of the Sacrifice of Noah with medallions, a detail   *On the side:* Ignudo above Prophet Jeremiah

PROPHETS AND SIBYLS

Twelve characters sit on mighty thrones flanked by monochrome putti in the external fascia: they are some Prophets and Sibyls. In the History of Israel, Prophets kept alive the hope of the Saviour's coming; in the profane world, the Sibyls are the idea and the waiting of redemption for mankind. Prophets and Sibyls represent a wait for the Redemption.

PROPHET JEREMIAS

His thoughtful face and worried attitude, but over all the two disconsolate figures behind him, underline the distinctive features that Jeremias embodies: the suffering for the future of the people of Israel far from Jerusalem. He is the prophet of the new alliance as well. The redemption of the people he tells is a sign of the deeper redemption that the Messiah will sanction.

The Persian Sybil

The name "Sybil" has not a proper ethimology in the classical tradition, and it indicates a young virgin woman who tells the future when she is inspired by a god, usually Apollo.

In the legend that is related to Sibyls the tradition wants some very old aged. Michelangelo among the five he paints, represents two of them, the Persian and the Cumaen Sibyls, with their faces hardly marked by time. Michelangelo paints the Persian Sybil like a myopic who tries to understand what he is reading. The feature of the images, notwithstanding the executive rapidity, is extremely accurate. Michelangelo uses colours to give a body to the Sybil's tumultuous interior life. Michelangelo decides to draw near contrasting colours on wide surfaces.

PROPHET EZEKIEL

Ezekiel is the prophet who lived at the time of the siege in Jerusalem and of the exile of Babylon. His mission is to herald the punishment to the people of Israel when the people were unfaithful to God, but to proclaim the conversion too, to the return of the alliance with God. Michelangelo gets in admirable synthesis all of these aspects in the re-alization of the Prophet's vigorous figure. Everything is centered on that attentive and worried face. The Angel on the background is also very beautiful. In his gesture, the right hand lifted up and the left one in a horizontal position, is the meaning of every prophetic vocation: listen to the Divinity telling the people.

ERYTHREAN SYBIL

According to the mythological legend the Sybil was born in a Grotto at Eritre, a locality in Lydia, region of Asia Minor. Apollo let her live as many years as she had grains of salt in her hand. Michel- angelo paints her turning over the pages of the book behind her shoulders. The gentle Sybil's face is exalted by the putto that lights a torch and can be considered an allusion to divine inspiration.

PROPHET JOEL

St. Peter mentions Prophet Joel's book on the day of Pentecost (in the first speech on the day of the first people meeting in Jerusalem) (Atti, 2,17-21) and links what has just happened in the supper room with the prophecy, the Holy Spirit's descent over the Virgin Mary and the Apostles."I give my Spirit to men and your sons and daughters will be prophets" (Joel 3, 1). Joel is therefore the prophet of the Pentecost.

Joel is the prophet of the restoration of Israel as well. He sees a vision of salvation for all of mankind, not only for his people.

PROPHET ZECHARIAH

Zechariah is a Messianic prophet. Matthew the Evangelist mentions his book from chapter 21: Jesus enters Jerusalem in a triumph.
The humble Jesus' mount should reveal the humble and pacific characteristic of the Messianic kingdom. In Zechariah's gesture, Michelangelo paints him turning over the pages of a book looking for new pages and is expressed in the idea we relate to the prophets; they are those who can anticipate future.

DELPHIC SYBIL

It is one of the most famous figures of the cycle because of its beauty. Michelangelo paints her standing on her bust and her head turned forward in an imperious gesture. Her eyes stare right as if from there divine inspiration should come. Her lively attitude is underlined by the curve of the papyrus she holds and by the wide swirl of the mantle. The famous Apollo's sanctuary and oracle, where the Sybil was charged to let the oracles know is in Delphi, Greece.

PROPHET ISAIAH

The prophets painted by Michelangelo all round the history of humanity from the creation to the sin, symbolize the wait for the redemption in the history of Israel's people. Isaiah is the most significant prophet about this story of hope.
Michelangelo catches him in the moment when he projects his sight through the vision of the new-born Messiah, while the Spirit's blow that takes him shakes his mantle. The little angel behind his shoulders revives the whole scene. His stretched arm seems to point out the realization of the plan for the redemption, to Isaiah.

CUMAEN SYBIL

When Michelangelo paints the Sibyls, he wants to underline the link between classical culture and Christianity. The Cumaen Sybil more than the other Sibyls links this. In the Aeneid by Virgil, the Cumaen Sybil confides Aeneas the prophecy about a baby born from a Virgin that had given an age of peace and happiness to mankind, as Prophet Isaiah wrote (Isaiah 7,14). Ancients Christians saw an allusion to Jesus' birth in this prophecy. It's not a case that Isaiah and the Cumaen Sybil are painted in the ceiling of the Sistine Chapel one next to the other.

PROPHET DANIEL

Prophet Daniel like Jonas is often represented in the paleochristian art. Daniel is let down in a ditch with hungry lions. Miraculously he doesn't die and the same king who wanted to kill him says: "Daniel's God is the everlasting God". (Daniel 6, 7).
Daniel is the prophet of the vision about "man's son" that is coming to judge people. Jesus says he is "Man's Son" (Matthew 8, 20), to underline what is clear in the prophet's book, that his kingdom is not related to time. Michelangelo paints him in the moment he is counting, with a strange instrument, the "seventy weeks" before the Saviour's coming (Daniel 9,24).

DANIEL

LIBYAN SYBIL

She is turning to put away and close her huge book. Michelangelo paints her like a young lady dressed in an unusual golden-yellow dress that leaves her shoulders completely naked. She turns her eyes down and the delicate twisting move- ment seems to have its pin on her legs. The legs are covered by a soft white veil that lets us catch a glimpse of her bodily vigour. Michelangelo puts together violet, orange, pink and yellow and the result is a wise and perfect combination of hues.

Prophet Jonas

Jonas is one of the most represented characters in the paleochristian art. The idea that Jonas was swallowed up by a big fish and after three days thrown back alive on a strand, had for sure hit the powerful imagination of the artists. Christ in the Gospel according to St. Matthew (12, 40) mentions Jonas' episode and considers it a fore-cast of his death and resurrection; resurrection that happens three days after the burial.

Michelangelo paints the prophet flanked by a big fish in the moment in which he accepts the mission to preach the people of Nineveh the necessity to repent their sins, be converted and make penance.

LUNETTES

Christ's ancestors from Abraham to Joseph, Maria's husband, according to the list that Matthew does in his Gospel are painted in the lunettes (1, 1-17).

These paintings are accounted for among Michelangelo's paintings. However without Jesus' genealogy the vault should miss a fundamental chapter. Michelangelo's idea is clear: the history of humanity moves in a project of salvation.

God's will to redeem his people takes birth from the first man, Adam and his sin, and develops generation by generation. The story of the vault and its characters' harmonize and complete in the ancestors' series. The previous sixteen lunettes were cut down to fourteen by Michelangelo. He was obliged to eliminate the two lunettes on the altar wall to give space to the Last Judgment.

Every lunette has in the center a table with the subject's names according to the genealogy at the beginning of the Gospel according to Matthew.

THE "PENNACCHI"

Michelangelo paints four triangular spaces in the corners of the Chapel: they are the so called "pennacchi", where Michelangelo paints important episodes of the history from Israelites. They are the fullness of the salvation that will be realized in God's Son that becomes man.

The brazen serpent
(biblical refer, Book of the Numbers, 21, 4-9)
God sends poisonous serpents as a punishment for his people, because of a new rebellion, and they kill a large number of Jews. Moses prays God and the Lord tells him to make a brazen serpent and to place it on the top of a spear so that "when a snake bites a person, if he looks the brazen snake he won't die" (Numbers 24,8)

The crucifixion of Amman
(biblical refer, Book of Ester, 3,9)
The episode painted by Michelangelo is from the Book of Ester. Ester was the Jew queen, married to the Persian king Xerxes, who succeeded to avoid a conspiracy against the Jews. Aman, esteemed King's confident, obtained an ordinance to exterminate the Jews with false declarations; and he tried to indict the Jew Mardocheo as a traitor. Es-

ter discovers the truth and obtains the revocation of the persecution. Aman is killed and tied to the same stake he prepared for Mardocheo.

David and Goliath
(biblical refer, Book of Samuel 17, 1-54)
The episode is famous, David defeats Goliath, Philistines' champion; the Philistines are the eternal enemies of Israel. It's imagined with few essential elements: a giant's colossal body lies on the ground, David is going to cut his enemy's head and in the close up we have the sling that David used to throw the stone to Goliath. The message is clear: God is Almighty; a young and unpractised man as David can win if he enjoys God's confidence.

Judith and Holofernes
(Biblical refer, book of Judith, 10-13)
The young and beautiful widow won the regard of Holofernes' confidence thanks to a strategy. He was the general of Assur's army, and after a long siege is going to defeat Israel's army. Judith kills him cutting his head. Once again God is the Almighty Lord, who cares about his people's destinies and uses what is little and humble to show his Highness and Benevolence.

THE "VELE"

In the triangular paintings, the "vele", are represented domestic groups related to Christ's ancestors painted in the lunettes down below. They are compressed in narrow and not profound spaces. Men and women represent humanity and the succession of generations. They wait, in different positions, the great event of the Revelation: they look tired, suffering and exasperated because of the long inactivity and because of the very slow passing time; time that divides them from the Saviour's birth. Michelangelo draws the domestic groups while they spend their life thinking of bodily thoughts. Their only function is procreation, that's why they are often represented taking care of their children, who are the first aim in their life and significantly their vocation.

The "vele" are surmounted with enigmatical bronze naked figures. They are painted in symmetrical postures obtained with the original preparatory cartoon, they show in the middle bucranes (oxen's skulls), classical ornamental motive that refer, in ancient times, to the sacrifices.

THE LAST JUDGEMENT

In 1533 Michelangelo had the commission, by Pope Clement VII (1523-1534) to paint the end-wall of the Sistine, twenty years later after the ceiling. The works started only in 1536, under Clement VII's successor Paul III (1534-1549) and finished in 1541, when with a magnificent celebration, on October 31, the beautiful fresco was discovered. The first decision by Michelangelo is to cover the wall with a wall made out of brick slightly bent towards the room (26cm), so that dust should not lodge on the fresco. Michelangelo destroys frescoes of the previous century and the lunettes he himself had painted, to have more room for his new fresco. Michelangelo reveals his culture in the Last Judgement. He knows very well the Bible and the "Divina Commedia" by Dante Alighieri, the work that can be considered the "sum" of medieval culture.

The artist's originality shows itself in an idea that has nothing to do with the classical schemes and in the solutions that many of his contemporaries were baffled about.

Angels without wings, saints without aureole, ugly devils beyond every imagination, everything is a warning on the vanity of the things and the irreversibility of the Judgement.

The complex iconography and the body's swinging in the different interlacings have their focal center in the almond made of light in the center and above all in the figure that together with his Mother occupies it at all. Mankind's Son that comes over the clouds of the sky and his imperious gesture bring the facts of the history to the truth. It's the moment of truth where things must show their own actual nature.

On the left the Resurrection of the dead is represented. The defuncts are attracted by an irresist-
ible force; they slowly stand up again and ascend
up to the sky. Some are still skeletons wrapped
up in the sudarium, others have already gained
their body.

The colour of their skin is deathly pale and their
faces express the dramatic situation.
The souls in bliss that have again a complete
bodily consistence start their ascent to heaven,
while their bodies and their robes find again
their lost colours.

An interesting detail is where two saints hanging to a rosary are lifted up to heaven by an angel. Perhaps Michelangelo wanted to underline the saving power of the prayer and particularly the power of the most traditional of the Christian popular prayers, the rosary in honour of the Virgin Mary diffused by San Domenico and his friars in the 14th century. The idea of the rosary is linked perhaps to the fact that Michelangelo was a votary to San Domenico, so that he worked in Bologna in 1494 to embellish the marble arch that still today preserves the relics of the saint.

Among the saints that crown Christ and the Virgin Mary some are recognizable because of the symbols related to the martyrdom, like the saints on the right of Christ: St. Andrew with the acute angle cross on his shoulder, St. John the Baptist with his muscular body and St Lawrence (bottom, by Mary's feet) who was slowly burned alive on a grill symbolized by the ladder that the saint has on his shoulder. The Saints like the other characters of the Last Judgement are painted with wide-open eyes and glances full to the brim with fear and expectation.

The two lunettes, that were previously dedicated to Christ's ancestors, in the higher section of the Judgement, are now animated by groups of angels without wings that bring the symbols of Passion. The Holy Cross towers in the lunette on the left, some angels in dramatic poses hold it with difficulty. On the right another group of angels holds the emblem of the martyr's crown, the Judeans used to crown the Saviour with.

Michelangelo follows the religious and spiritual culture of his time and glorifies in this lunette two of the most important signs of the *"passio Christi"*: the Holy Cross and the Crown. The column of the flagellation stands out in the lunette on the right. Up above you can notice an angel with a feminine face that seems to point at the column and with the other hand holds the sponge imbued with vinegar with which Christ quenched his thirst. Some critics have seen some resemblance with Vittoria Colonna, marquise of Pescara, whom Michelangelo knew during the years of the last Judgement and to whom he dedicated many poems. The angels that fly in the lunettes hold some symbols that refer to the nar-

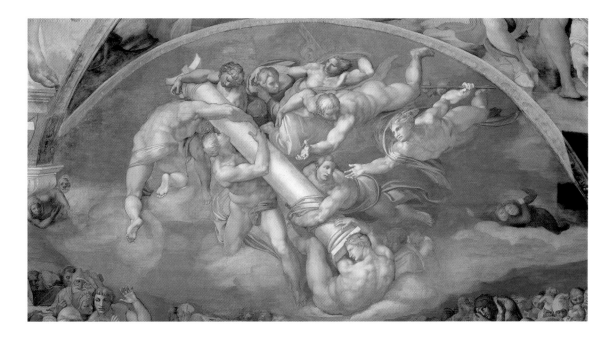

ration from the Gospel that you can find in the Synoptic Gospel.

The representation of Bartholomew is peculiar, he is painted with a knife in his hand and the other hand holds a human skin.

Tradition wants Saint Bartholomew to be skinned alive. The main characteristic of the painting is related to that vague face painted in the skin. Many critics have singled out Michel-angelo's self-portrait there.

Peter's figure stands out on Christ's left. You can recognize Saint Peter because he holds two keys. In another group of Saints, down below, always on Christ's left, you can recognize: Santa Caterina from Alessandria with the cog – wheel of her martyrdom and Saint Biagius with the ironcomb of his torture; Saint Sebastian is nearby on his knees holding the arrows.

It's difficult not to be impressed by the glances of the characters' faces in the Sistine Chapel. Their big eyes penetrate and let them be penetrated; they disclose the feelings and they are mirrors for the character's soul to which they belong. Man's terror and desperation when he is dragged down by the devil is summed up in that wide open eye, where Michelangelo centres the maximum of the woe and in the half-open mouth hidden by the hand that increases the sense of desperation and the ineluctable punishment.

The scene with Charon, the mythological ferryman, as main character is noteworthy. Michelangelo's Charon doesn't ferry the damned souls, but pushes damned souls out the boat toward Hell, and forsakes them to their dramatic destiny.

The group ends with Biagio da Cesena's figure, he was the Master of Ceremonies of the Pope and he judged Michelangelo's work worthy to stay in a bathroom or in a tavern. The artist paints him in the features of Minos, one of the judges of Hell in the Greek-Roman mythology. He is the one who points the damned souls out, through the number of the serpent coils on his body, the circle where they have to go.

After the decision of the Council of Trent (1563) where they decided to let only works of art with "decorum" according to the Holy Scriptures in the holy space execute, the frescoes of the Last Judgement were "retouched" by a Michelangelo's scholar, Daniel da Volterra. He painted veils and girdles to cover the nudity of the figures. Some other "retouchings" were executed later. In the last restoration they have left the painting by Daniel da Volterra as a testimony of that history. Today the Chapel opens once again in its whole splendour "to testify the beauty of man created by God" and "the true sanctuary of the theology of the human body" (Giovanni Paolo II, Homely, April 8, 1994).

The pieces from the Bible are from "The Bible of Jerusalem", Bologna 1999. The most known versions at Michelangelo's time were the "Vulgata", I it's an edition in vulgar Latin by San Girolamo (390-405), that was the most known text for the west-world. The first translation in Italian was by Nicolò Malermi and was published in 1741.

MICHELANGELO

Michelangelo or the "sublime genius". It is virtually impossible for men and women of our generation to escape the awesome influence of a critical history that has conditioned us for centuries.

The adjective "sublime" (or the no less peremptory "terrible" or "divine") has been attributed to Michelangelo since the time of Ascanio Condivi and Giorgio Vasari, his contemporaries. In the opening words of the biography of Michelangelo Buonarroti in Vasari's "Lives" we read: "...the most benignant rector of Heaven cast his merciful eyes towards the earth and... decided to send into the world an artist who would be skilled in every art and craft, whose work would serve to show us how to achieve perfection in art – in drawing and in the use of contour, in using light and shadow to create relief in painting – and to use judgement in sculpture, and, in architecture, make dwellings safe, comfortable, healthy, pleasant, well-proportioned and rich in ornament. He determined, moreover, to give this artist a knowledge of true moral philosophy and the gift of poetry, so that the world might admire him and take him as a model in life, in work, in manners and in all human actions; so that he may be called divine rather than earthly".

The process of deification has already taken place. The birth of Michelangelo is not a mere human birth, but an "epiphany", a divine manifestation. The imposition of his style is the epoch-making event that concludes – having reached a peak of perfection that will and can never be surpassed – the centuries old labour of the arts: Michelangelo is thus "divine rather than earthly". This is how he is described by Vasari. We are given a similar description by Ascanio Condivi, his favourite pupil, whose reverential admiration appears misted and softened by affection. His "Life" begins thus:"From the moment that God, in his beneficence, granted me the honour not only of enjoying the presence (into which I scarcely hoped to come), but also the affection, the conversation and the intimate friendship of that rare painter and sculptor, Michelangelo Buonarroti...". Condivi talks of his friendship with the artist in terms of a mystical experience, an ineffable privilege. From the beginning the myth of Michelangelo grew up around the idea of the unique, the extraordinary, the "other", as we see from this brief critical anthology: "I am so enthusiastic about Michelangelo that not even Nature can satisfy me after him, for I cannot see her with his eyes" (Goethe, Italian Journey); "The only sentiment that divinity can inspire in feeble mortals is terror: and Michelangelo seems born on purpose

Michelangelo, Piety,
Basilica of St Peter, Vatican City

to stamp this fear in the soul..." (Stendhal, Roman Walk); "From the first moment Michelangelo was a total personality, almost frightening in his single-mindedness" (Wölfflin 1899). Michelangelo god or "titan". Thus, a critical idea that started with Vasari and Condivi, ably assisted by the artist himself during his lifetime with his absolutely exceptional existential and literary behaviour, has been handed down to us, influencing the thought and actions of millions of people. For a public from all over the world, Michelangelo represents today a "fatal attraction". No other artist of the past, neither Raphael nor Rembrandt or even Leonardo da Vinci enjoys such a vast, acritical and unconditioned consensus. And it is certainly not a coincidence that Michelangelo's sculpture-symbols (the "Pieta" in St. Peter's in Rome and the "David" in the Accademia in Florence) have been, in recent years, the victims of senseless vandalism. In a certain sense these episodes are the direct result of the myth. The "Stendhal syndrome" has shown its dark side. All this, if we consider it carefully, stems from the critical (and museographical) interpretation of Michelangelo that has historically been given. Take, for example, the present collocation of the "David" in its 19th century museum setting in the Accademia. The statue has an almost liturgical collocation as the altar of the Eucharist in a church; it stands, isolated in its awesome beauty, in the centre of the tribune-apse, in the zenithal light that comes from the skylight, like the tabernacle of the Holy Sacrament. Its image is immediately given a kind of secular consecration until it takes on, in the collective imagination, the propitiatory and ritual function of a divinity. Since the gods govern the absolute and the irrational, and since they are objects of love and (more

rarely) hate, the logical consequence is the violent dialogue between the madman and the god – a god created by art historians. Are the criticisms directed against the restoration (moreover accurate) of the Sistine Chapel ceiling not the consequence of a critical myth that the cleaning has helped to put in crisis? We were used to thinking of Michelangelo in terms of black and white, the colours typical of the "terrible" or "sublime", and now, perhaps, we are disappointed by the bright, acid colours of the Mannerist palette, so close to Pontormo and Rosso and, thus, so firmly placed in historical perspective. The point is that, when we face the question of Michelangelo, the real problem lies in overcoming the ahistorical or metahistorical tangent that for centuries has oriented the interpretation of his personality.

Michelangelo, David,
Academy Gallery, Florence

Daniele da Volterra, Bust of Michelangelo,
Academy Gallery, Florence

THE LIFE OF MICHELANGELO

Michelangelo was born on 6 March 1475, at Caprese in the Casentino between Arezzo and Chiusi, where his father, Lodovico di Leonardo Buonarroti (1446-1531) held the post of "podestà". The artist's mother was Francesca di Neri (1455-1481), a Florentine. In 1488 a young friend, the Florentine painter, Francesco Granacci (1469-1543) introduced Michelangelo to Domenico Ghirlandaio in whose important workshop he was given a three-year contract of apprenticeship. During this period he made copies of frescoes by Giotto and Masaccio (some drawings are in collections in Paris, Louvre; Munich, Staatliche Graphische Sammlung; Vienna, Albertina) and painted a panel (now lost) of the "Temptation of St. Anthony", inspired by an engraving by the German painter, Martin Schongauer (c. 1440-1494). Leaving Ghirlandaio's shop before the end of his contract, Michelangelo went in 1489 to work in the Medici gardens of the convent of San Marco in Florence where the sculptor, Bertoldo di Giovanni (c. 1440-1491), ran a school for young artists under the direct protection of Lorenzo the Magnificent and interested mainly in the study of classical sculpture. The young Michelangelo was invited by Lorenzo himself to reside in the Medici Palace, where he came into contact with the major figures of Florentine Humanism,

including Agnolo Poliziano, Marsilio Ficino, the most important Platonic thinker – a philosophy in which Michelangelo maintained a firm belief throughout his life – and Cristoforo Landino, a scholar of Dante, whose poetry Michelangelo always loved. Michelangelo's first works in sculpture date from the early part of the last decade of the Quattrocento. In October 1494 the artist hurriedly left Florence which was about to be invaded by the army of Charles VIII. He went first to Bologna, then Venice, returning almost immediately to Bologna where he stayed for a year, working on the three sculptures for the tomb of St. Dominic in the church of the same name. During his first stay in Rome between 1496 and 1501, Michelangelo is recorded as having made a cartoon (now lost) for a painting of "St. Francis Receiving the Stigmata", destined for the church of St. Peter in Montorio but never painted. During this period he made the statue of "Bacchus", now in the Bargello in Florence and the "Pietà" in St. Peter's in the Vatican. When he returned to Florence in the spring of 1501, he was given numerous commissions for works of sculpture, including the "David", now in the Galleria dell'Accademia. In 1504 he was given the important commission of painting the fresco of the "Battle of Cascina", alongside Leonardo's "Battle of Anghiari" in the Council Chamber of Palazzo Vecchio in Florence. Three "tondi" also date from the first decade of the Cinquecento, two in sculpture and one painted on panel, known as the "Doni Tondo" (Florence, Uffizi). In March 1505 Julius II commissioned Michelangelo to make a project for his monumental tomb. This work was to prove a real 'tragedy' for the artist who successively abandoned the project and took it up again over the next forty years, finally only partially completing it.

In May 1508 work started on the frescoes for the Sistine Chapel ceiling. The total secrecy and solitude with which Michelangelo completed the work in October 1512 is perhaps the most typical aspect of the life of this extraordinary man, and totally different to that of the other artistic genius of early Cinquecento Rome, Raphael Sanzio, who exploited to a maximum the 'wordly' aspects of his work.

In the following years the artist worked mainly in Florence, where the Medici had returned to power in 1512, and where he completed to a greater or lesser extent his great architectural and

Birthplace of Michelangelo in Caprese, near Arezzo

Michelangelo, Rondanini Piety, Sforza Castle, Milan

Michelangelo, The Holy Family with St John
(Doni Roundel), Uffizi Gallery, Florence

sculptural projects: the facade of the church of San Lorenzo, the Laurentian Library, the Medici Chapel or New Sacristy in San Lorenzo. In 1530 he painted a "Leda" for Duke Alfonso d'Este of Ferrara, then giving it, however, to Antonio Mini who took it to France where it was lost. In the winter of 1532-33 Michelangelo was in Rome where he became friends with the nobleman Tommaso de' Cavalieri, a friendship that was to last until his death. The artist painted for him a series of mythological drawings (London, British Museum; Windsor, Royal Library). The cartoon of "Noli me tangere", made for Alfonso d'Avalos. also dates from the 1530s; the cartoon is now lost but we have copies by Bronzino and Pontormo, who also made a painting (Florence, Uffizi) from another cartoon, "Venus and Cupid" (1532-34).

In the spring of 1536 Michelangelo started work on the grandiose fresco of the "Last Judgement" on the altar wall of the Sistine Chapel; it was finished in November 1541. Shortly after Paul III commissioned the frescoes for the Pauline Chapel in the Vatican, painted between 1542 and 1550. In his old age Michelangelo received much support, particularly spiritual, from his great friendship with the marchesa Vittoria Colonna (1490-1547), for whom he painted a "Christ crucified with mourners", now lost, but for which we have the preparatory drawing (London, British Museum).

Michelangelo continued to work up until a few days before his death on the "Rondanini Pietà" (Milan, Castello Sforzesco). He died on 18 February 1564, at about four thirty in the afternoon, after being in bed for only two days. His friend, Tommaso de' Cavalieri who "he loved more than any other" (Vasari) was with him, together with Daniele da Volterra and a few others. The body was taken to the church of Santi Apostoli; the Pope wanted him buried in St. Peter's but his nephew, Leonardo Buonarroti, had the body brought back to Florence where it arrived on March 10th and was buried in the church of Santa Croce. A memorial service was held on July 14th in the church of San Lorenzo.

Giorgio Vasari, Tomb of Michelangelo,
Basilica of Santa Croce, Florence

In the pages that follow:
The Sistine Chapel, external view

Bibliography

G. Vasari, *Le vite dei più eccellenti pittori, scultori e architetti, nelle redazioni del 1550 e 1568*, a cura di R. Bettarini e P. Barocchi, Firenze 1987; C. de Tolnay, *Michelangelo II, The Sistine Ceiling*, Princeton 1945; R. Pane, *L'architettura della Volta Sistina*, in A.A. V.V., Michelangiolo Architetto, Torino 1964; A.A. V.V., *La Cappella Sistina in Vaticano*, Milano 1965; A.A. V.V., *Biblioteca Sanctorum*, Roma 1966; D. Redig de Campos, I *"tituli" degli affreschi del Quattrocento nella Cappella Sistina*, in "Rendiconti della Pontificia Accademia Romana di Archeologia", XLII, 1969-70; A.A. V.V., *La Cappella Sistina. I primi restauri: la scoperta del colore*, Novara 1986; J. Shearman, *La Cappella Sistina*, Novara 1986; K. Hartt, G. Colalucci, F. Mancinelli, *La Cappella Sistina. I, La Preistoria della Bibbia. II, Gli Antenati di Cristo. III, La Storia della Creazione*, Milano 1990; A.A. V.V., *Michelangelo e la Sistina. La tecnica, il restauro, il mito*, Roma 1990; R. de Maio, *Michelangelo e la Controriforma*, Firenze 1990; S. Moltedo (a cura di) *La Sistina riprodotta. Gli affreschi di Michelangelo dalle stampe del Cinquecento alle campagne fotografiche Anderson*, Città del Vaticano 1991; A.A. V.V., *La Cappella Sistina. La volta restaurata: il trionfo del colore*, Novara 1992; A. Aletta (a cura di), *Conversazioni sotto la Volta. La nuova volta della Cappella Sistina e il Manierismo romano fino al 1550*, Roma 1992; F. Mancinelli, A. M. de Strobel, *Michelangelo. Le Lunette e le Vele della Cappella Sistina*, Roma 1992; C. Lewin, *The Sistine Chapel walls and the Roman Liturgy*, The Pennsylvania State University 1993; F. Mancinelli, *La Cappella Sistina*, Edizioni Musei Vaticani 1994; F. Mancinelli, G. Colalucci, N. Gabrielli, *Michelangelo. Il Giudizio Universale*, in Art Dossier all. al n. 88, Firenze 1994; P. de Vecchi, *La Cappella Sistina. Il retauro degli affreschi di Michelangelo*, Milano 1996; E. Calvesi, *La Cappella Sistina e la sua decorazione da Perugino a Michelangelo*, Roma 1997; L. Partridge, F. Mancinelli, G. Colalucci, *La Cappella Sistina. Il Giudizio restaurato*, Novara 1998; G. Vasari, *La vita di Michelangelo nelle redazioni del 1550 e del 1568*, a cura di P. Barocchi, vol. I, Milano-Napoli, 1962; A. Condivi, *Vita di Michelangelo Buonarroti*, Roma, 1553; a cura di P. d'Ancona, Milano, 1928; C. de Tolnay, *Michelangelo, I-V*, Princeton, N.J., 1943-1960; P. Barocchi, *Michelangelo e la sua scuola: i disegni di Casa Buonarroti e degli Uffizi*, Firenze, 1962; AA.VV., *Michelangelo architetto*, a cura di P. Portoghesi e B. Zevi, Torino, 1964; P. Barocchi-R. Ristori, *Il Carteggio di Michelangelo*, I-IV, Firenze, 1965-1979; L. Goldscheider, *Michelangelo*, London-New York. 1967; C. de Tolnay, *Corpus dei disegni di Michelangelo*. I-IV, Novara, 1971-1980; AA.VV., *La Cappella Sistina. I primi restauri: la scoperta del colore*, Novara, 1986; F. Mancinelli, *Il cantiere di Michelangelo per la volta della Cappella Sistina*, in "La pittura in Italia. Il Cinquecento", tomo II, Milano, 1988, pp. 535-552; AA.VV., *La Cappella Sistina. La volta restaurata: il trionfo del colore*, Novara, 1992.

Ats Italia Editrice s.r.l.
Via di Brava, 41/43 - 00163 Roma
Largo M. Liverani, 12/3 - 50141 Firenze
www.atsitalia.it

Editorial coordination: *Frida Giannini*
Image research: *Angela Giommi*
Graphic design, layout and cover: *Valeria Li Causi*
Scanning and colour correction: *Leandro Ricci*
Technical coordination: *Flavio Zancla, Valerio Petrucci*

Text:
Prof. *Sonia Gallico*
Scheda *"Michelangelo"* by Antonio Paolucci
Profilo biografico di Michelangelo by Angelo Tartuferi
Scheda *"I restauro degli affreschi della Cappella Sistina"* by Fabrizio Mancinelli

Photographs:
Foto Servizio Fotografico dei Musei Vaticani © Musei Vaticani
Archivio ATS Italia Editrice s.r.l.
Archivio fotografico Fabbrica di San Pietro in Vaticano
Archivio Foto Scala, Firenze

Printworks: Papergraf - Piazzola sul Brenta (PD)